This book belongs to:

A. Rexon

This 1989 Muppet Press book is published by Longmeadow Press.
Distributed by Checkerboard Press,
a division of Macmillan, Inc.

Printed in United States
ISBN 002-689262-6
a b c d e f g h

Adding Fraggles

by Bonnie Worth   illustrated by Larry Di Fiori

Muppet Press

One little Fraggle, lazing in the sun.

Zero comes to join him...

So there's just **one.**

1

+ 0
———

1

One little Fraggle, tying his shoe.

One comes to help him…

$$+1$$

And now there are **two.**

2

Two little Fraggles, climbing a tree.

2

One brings a ladder…

+ 1
___

And now there are **three.**

3

Three little Fraggles, knocking on a door.

3

One comes to answer…

+ 1

And now there are **four.**

4

Four little Fraggles, lining up to dive.

One brings some towels…

And now there are **five.**

Five little Fraggles, beating on sticks.

5

One brings a horn…

+1

And now there are **six.**

6

Now that you are up to six, here are some terrific tricks!

Three jogging Fraggles plus **two** more

Is the same as **one** biker added to **four.**

5

5

No matter which way they arrive,
The sum of each group is still **five.**

2 + 4 =

Two plus **four,** racing madly up a hill,

5 + 1 =

Or **five** plus **one**—sitting perfectly still…

6

6

The groups are split up differently,
But both add up to **six,** you see!

A really nifty number game
Is adding two that are the same.   Try it!

One   and   **one**   are

Two   and   **two**   are

2

two.

four.

That's very good so far!
Ready to try more?

Three   and   **three**   are

Four   and   **four**   are

6

six.

8

That's even better now.
You're doing simply great!

eight.

5 + 5 =

Five and **five** are

10 + 10 =

Ten and **ten** are

10
ten.

20
twenty.

You've really learned a lot. Up to twenty's plenty!
Can you turn back, right to the start,
And learn these adding games by heart?